Work Readiness™

great interpersonal skills

michael a. sommers

ROSEN
PUBLISHING®

New York

Published in 2008 by The Rosen Publishing Group, Inc.
29 East 21st Street, New York, NY 10010

First Edition

Library of Congress Cataloging-in-Publication Data

Sommers, Michael A., 1966–
Great interpersonal skills / Michael A. Sommers.
    p. cm.—(Work readiness)
Includes bibliographical references and index.
ISBN-13: 978-1-4042-1423-1 (hardcover)
1. Organizational behavior—Juvenile literature. 2. Interpersonal relations—Juvenile literature. 3. Interpersonal communication—Juvenile literature. I. Title.
HD58.7.S676 2008
650.1'3—dc22

                                                                    2007023663

Manufactured in the United States of America

contents

Unless you live in a cave or on a deserted island, you can't avoid interacting with other people. You may not even think about it, but your life is shaped by the daily contact you have with everybody from family members, friends, and strangers to teachers, coaches, and even crossing guards. Meanwhile, if you've ever had a part-time or summer job, you've also discovered how important it is to get along well with your coworkers and superiors. Even if you work on your own—you have a paper route, for example—having a good relationship with your customers is essential if you want your job to go smoothly.

Introduction

The truth is that no matter what kind of job you might have, two—or more—heads are often better than one. It doesn't matter how your ideas or personality may differ from those of your coworkers. Learning to exchange viewpoints, solve problems, and work in teams or groups is crucial. Of course, that doesn't mean it's always easy. For example, what do you do when a colleague is bossy, or never wants to share credit or listen to what you have to say? How do you react to the good-humored slacker who is a great pal but doesn't pull her weight when the pressure is on? And how do you deal with a manager who plays favorites?

Getting along and communicating well with coworkers doesn't necessarily happen automatically. Abilities known as interpersonal skills are needed. Some people naturally possess good interpersonal skills. Many others discover that they have to work at it to deal productively with others. It's all the more challenging when you find yourself in a job setting where people have different personalities and backgrounds. Learning to adapt and deal positively with these and other types of people in order to get the job done is what acquiring good interpersonal skills is all about.

The ability to work well with others depends upon understanding and appreciating people's differences. It also involves using these differences to your best advantage—in order to make your job easier and more satisfying. Fortunately, interpersonal skills can be learned by anybody. All it takes is awareness, patience, and practice.

No matter what kind of job you have, if people are involved, then having good interpersonal skills will take you far. Employers increasingly place value on workers who get along with people at all levels, from the mailroom staff to the president. Ultimately, this is to an employer's advantage: having employees who work harmoniously together not only makes for a happier, healthier work environment but also for a more productive and profitable one as well.

chapter one

EFFECTIVE COMMUNICATION

In the most basic day-to-day sense, communicating is something we do every time we open our mouths to speak. At our jobs, communication often consists of talking to someone in person, on the phone, or via webcam. It might also involve writing a letter, e-mail, or instant message (IM). Whether communication is done face-to-face or via cyberspace, the goal is to share information.

Although we communicate all the time, it is not necessarily as straightforward as it might seem. In order to get a point across in an effective and positive way, you need to think about what, why, and how you're communicating. You also need to think about with whom you're communicating. Whether you're providing instruction, asking a question, or firing off a quick e-mail, the message that you send is not always the message that the person on the other end receives.

Verbal and Nonverbal Communication

Effective verbal communication requires clear and unambiguous language. You don't want people to have to

Communicating involves more than just speech. Hand and facial gestures can also convey many different meanings.

assume or guess what point you are trying to make. It can help to think about what you want to say and prepare before you speak.

What another person understands or concludes from your words can vary enormously based not only on what you say and the language you use but also on many other factors, too. In fact, a large percentage of daily communication is nonverbal. If you're speaking face-to-face, the person or people you're talking with will take in such details as your facial expressions, body language, and posture. They will also pick up on aspects of

This man's body language suggests that he is feeling defensive and ill at ease.

vocal communication that are separate from your actual words. This includes factors such as voice tone, loudness, and inflection—all of which can significantly affect the meaning of what you are saying. When something is said in a strong tone, for example, listeners might interpret enthusiasm and confidence. The same words spoken in a hesitant tone might convey lack of interest or insecurity.

Suppose that you're talking while shuffling your feet, staring out the window, and mumbling. All of these factors will have a big effect not only on how you're perceived but also on what you're communicating. You'll sound as if you don't know what you're talking about. On the other hand, imagine speaking in a calm, firm voice while looking people in the eye, smiling, and exhibiting good posture. Chances are the same message will not only be more clearly heard but will also seem more impressive and authoritative.

If you're communicating via telephone, the person or people you're talking with can't see you. Nonetheless, they will still be able to make judgments about you based on such details as the volume and tone of your voice. And

Think Before You "Send"

In their book *Send: The Essential Guide to Email for Office and Home*, David Shipley and Will Schwalbe discuss how unclear or carelessly worded e-mail messages can lead to big-time personal, financial, and even legal problems for both senders and receivers. They summarize their e-mail experiences with two pieces of advice: (1) Send e-mails that you would like to receive and (2) think before you send.

The problem with e-mail is that you can screw up even before you actually start writing your message. Common—and potentially disastrous—mistakes of this sort include addressing the e-mail to the wrong recipients. Misusing the "Bcc" and "Forward" commands can result in a highly confidential message being sent to hundreds of people!

these judgments will affect how they perceive you—as well as the message you are trying to get across. If during a phone conversation with your boss, for example, you sound impatient or in a rush, it won't matter what you're saying. Your boss will likely think you're not paying attention or are not interested in the subject under discussion. He or she may grow annoyed. However, if you speak to your boss calmly, using an enthusiastic tone and encouraging questions and feedback, your conversation will be much more successful and agreeable for both of you.

The Written Word

Increasingly, more and more people are using e-mail and text messaging to communicate. You might think that with

At work, e-mailing has become so second nature that we often send a message without reading it over first. This can lead to messages being misinterpreted.

written messages, there is less room for misinterpretations. In reality, though, with e-mail people tend to focus on small details even more. Spelling mistakes, for example, can undermine the content of your message. They're the written equivalent of staring out the window while giving an oral report or speaking in a whisper while delivering a speech. Other details can also affect your communication. For instance, the way you sign off can have an impact on the entire content of your e-mail. "See ya" might seem too familiar or even rude in a situation where you barely know somebody. Meanwhile, signing "Best" might seem hurried or perhaps distant if sent to someone with whom you've been working closely for some time.

Receiving Messages

Communication is a two-way street. Many people are great talkers. However, the ability to listen well is a valuable skill. Being a good listener, or receiver, is about more than just hearing the words coming out of someone's mouth. It involves giving your full attention and really digesting a speaker's or writer's message. This is something you can't do if you're playing computer games while on the phone, for example, or listening to your iPod while reading an e-mail. In a face-to-face meeting, listening means looking directly at the speaker (unless you choose to take notes). Make sure you comprehend the message that is being given. If you don't, ask questions. If you can't hear or understand something, then politely ask the speaker to talk louder or slower, or to repeat himself or herself. It is your responsibility, just as much as his or hers, to make sure that the communication flows smoothly and that everybody fully understands the points being expressed.

Context

The context of what is being said is as important as the actual message. Context refers to the environment or situation in which communication takes place. Some situations might require more formal behavior, for example, that in another setting might seem stiff, awkward, or uncomfortable.

Many people increasingly resort to multitasking, in which they simultaneously perform—or at least try to—more than one activity at a time.

Distractions

You always need to consider the fact that any single message—particularly one sent and received during a busy workday—can be affected by distractions. Distractions can be external or internal. External distractions are those caused by the surrounding environment. Examples of such interruptions include disruptive telephone calls, people barging in to talk, and background noise such as passing traffic. In cases like these, the person you are speaking with may not be able to give you his or her

When colleagues work in cubicles or close quarters, there are many possible distractions that can be disruptive. Meanwhile, having a messy workspace can also be distracting.

undivided attention. External distractions can be difficult to control, but so can internal ones such as unwanted thoughts that keep creeping into your head, lack of sleep, or stress.

All of these factors can get in the way of communication. Therefore, it is best to do what you can to keep them to a minimum. For instance, if you're having an important conversation, turn off your cell phone. Hold a meeting in a quiet room, where everyone can focus, rather than in a busy area. And get enough sleep the night before a big conference so that you will be able to concentrate on effective communication.

Of course, it is harder to control whether the person you're talking with or writing to is distracted. If you sense someone is suffering from internal rather than external distractions, you can suggest moving to a calmer environment. Focus on speaking slowly and clearly with lots of eye contact. Ask questions to make sure the person understands everything you're saying and encourage feedback.

Friendly Atmosphere

Communication also flows well in a friendly, positive environment, where ideas can be shared without fear or resentment. This doesn't mean that you have to be best friends with everyone. But it does mean that you should always try to be professional and polite. How well or poorly you get along with other people can have a major impact on how messages are interpreted.

For instance, let's say you really don't like your boss because he's always on your case. One day, he comes up to you and criticizes some element of your work but goes on to compliment your overall performance. Instead of basking in your boss's praise, you're more likely to focus on his critical comments because they feed into your dislike for him. However, say you and a colleague have a relationship in which you always encourage and support each other. Because of the confidence and friendship you share, if there comes a time when you give her a tip on how she could improve at her job, she will probably really appreciate you telling her the truth. Not only will she listen to what you have to say (without becoming defensive), but she'll be more likely to follow your advice.

chapter two

Good Relationships

In your day-to-day life, you are constantly interacting with people you've known for a long time as well as those you might have just met. However, whether it's a teacher, coach, sibling, friend, or even someone on a Web site or chat room, these relationships don't just happen. They are formed based on what you—and the other people—put into them. As you grow older and gain more knowledge about the people in your life, your experiences will affect how you continue to deal with them—and with others, too.

Good relationships are an essential part of a happy and productive work environment. But how do you actually create these good relationships? In many circumstances, you have the freedom to choose with whom you want to hang out or collaborate. At a job, however, you often have no choice. Instead, you pretty much must get along with coworkers, some of whom may have very different personalities and ideas from your own. You may not even like some of them all that much. Getting around these differences and working together effectively is where interpersonal skills come in.

Managing Relationships

On any given day at your job, you may deal with just a couple of people, or you may deal with many: colleagues, managers, bosses, interns, customers, and delivery people. You don't need to like these people, but you do need to work with them. Moreover, you need to work well together. This involves more than just you doing your job while they do theirs and expecting that everything else will take care of itself. Often, working well with others depends upon your ability to manage relationships.

Learning how to handle relationships with coworkers is important because relationships need to develop in order to thrive. Like a garden, if left untended, they may fall into decay. If you ignore other people's needs and show no concern for their problems, your relationships with them will likely suffer. However, in well-managed relationships, people feel motivated and have a sense of comradery. This makes it easier to work toward a common goal.

Although you may not be aware of it, you very likely have had the experience of being "managed." Have you ever had a meeting with a coach or boss in which you came away feeling pleased that you were treated kindly and that your opinions were considered? Even if your boss or coach asked you to change certain things about your performance, did you still feel as if your efforts were appreciated? This is just one example of relationship management.

When you're treated well and encouraged to feel a connection with people, you're motivated to give your

No matter what kind of work you do, if you treat clients and customers with kindness and patience, you're much more likely to achieve successful results.

best. You also most likely look forward to dealing and working with these people. In addition, when you go out of your way to consider other people's needs, chances are they will want to cooperate with you and help you succeed as well.

Problem Relationships

Of course, sometimes you'll have to deal with people who have difficult attitudes or personalities. If you're

Yelling at someone is never a good way of communicating. Instead of resolving problems, it just creates new ones.

starting a new job, an employee who has been around for a long time might feel threatened by you. He might want to call all the shots or blame you whenever something goes wrong. Or a colleague might unfairly blame you because she was friends with the person who had the job before and was fired. For this reason, she might resent you or think you're doing everything wrong.

You may try to be polite to such coworkers and to talk to them about any problems they might have. Unfortunately, if these people are really difficult, your attempts might not be successful. Such situations can leave you feeling stressed, confused, and unmotivated to go to work. You may spend a lot of time hoping they will change, get transferred, or even fired so that you can actually look forward to work. However, wishing for change is a waste of time. No matter how much you might wish it, some people may never see your point of view. In the end, the only person you can ever change is yourself.

Unfortunately, in life, there will be many situations over which you'll have no control. But instead of being miserable, try to accept that there are times when you really *can't* be in control of a situation. However, although you can't be in control, you can be in charge.

In Control vs. In Charge

When you try to be in control, it means you are trying to get others to accept the way you think things should be. When that doesn't happen, you may feel frustrated or angry because others are keeping you from reaching your goal. In comparison, being in charge means that you accept a situation for what it is—not the way you wish it would be. Once you do this, you can work with and around any difficulties in your path to meet your goals as best you can.

In terms of managing relationships, being in charge means that when people are being difficult, you should try to see where they are coming from and why it is affecting you. Why are they behaving in this manner? What are their goals? (Oftentimes, conflict develops when people have different goals.) Then, look at your

Even if a client or colleague is upset or difficult to deal with, you can stay in charge of a situation if you stay calm, polite, and professional.

own attitudes. Are you able to see their points of view? Do you sympathize with their problems?

Once you have figured out what's really happening and why, you can try to manage the situation by making changes to the relationship. You can do this by attempting to get rid of or reduce negative aspects while concentrating on the good. For example, a coworker's extreme bossiness might get under your skin so much that you may tend to overlook the fact that she's creative and intelligent. By focusing on her great ideas and trying to

A Matter of Perspective

Sometimes, it is easier to focus on what's wrong rather than find something positive about a situation. Often, however, it's just a question of how you look at it. Try considering a problem from a different angle, such as in the following example:

Negative outlook: "I'm a twenty-year-old woman with barely any work experience. I work with men, many twice my age, who make me feel inferior and stupid. Before I even open my mouth, I find I have no confidence."

Positive outlook: "I'm an enthusiastic young woman who is willing to learn new things. I work with men, many twice my age, who can teach me a lot, but who are sometimes set in their ways. I find that when I speak up, I can offer a unique perspective as both a young person and a woman, which makes me a valuable member of this company."

downplay her bossiness, chances are you'll have a better and more productive relationship.

It can be quite productive to maintain perspective. For instance, if you work in the service industry—a restaurant or store, for example—don't let it get you down when customers complain. Instead, use the complaint as constructive criticism to provide even better service or do an even better job. Your efforts will not only prove to clients that you are listening to them but will also show that you are a professional.

While not every problem can be resolved, most can be improved. More important, by changing your attitude about a situation, not only will you feel better about your job and yourself, but others also will change the way they see you. Blaming others, making excuses, or getting angry or defensive doesn't improve a situation. If you concentrate on solutions instead of problems, however, obstacles can become opportunities.

chapter three

COOPERATION AND TEAMWORK

Today's workplace is increasingly complex. Instead of simple jobs that can be performed by one person, many projects require the talents and input of several individuals, each with their own special expertise and knowledge. For this reason, employers place enormous value on people who work well in teams or groups. It doesn't matter whether your job is in a restaurant or at a major international company: teamwork is often the most efficient, least expensive, and sometimes, only way to get a job done.

What Is a Team?

When you hear the word "team," you may immediately think of a sports team. On a soccer, volleyball, or basketball team, for example, all players are on the same side and their goal is to beat the opposition. Team members train together, learn to depend upon each other, and make the most of each player's particular skills and talents. When team members work well together, they are usually able to meet the goals set by their coach or manager.

In sports, all members of a team share the same goal. In the workplace, teamwork can be more complicated, especially when there isn't a clear goal in sight.

Although individual personalities or attitudes may cause occasional problems, the team itself is much more important than any one individual player.

Teams at Work

No matter what the sport, a team's goal—as well as that of all its players—is very clear: to score as much as possible to win. In the workplace, however, teamwork can be more complicated. People may want to play by their own rules and follow their own goals. Furthermore,

What a Team Is

Being part of a harmonious team not only makes it easier to accomplish projects but also makes for a happier work environment. When you're part of a well-functioning team, these are some of the advantages:

- You feel as if you're a part of things.
- You receive support and guidance from others.
- There is an exchange of opinions and ideas.
- Fewer mistakes are made.
- You—and those around you—will be more confident.

What a Team Isn't

There are some things a team doesn't have to be:

- People on a team don't have to be best buddies.
- Team members don't have to like or hang out with each other.
- Teams aren't for having group "therapy" sessions where everyone spills their personal problems.

although ideally there shouldn't be opposition among employees in a workplace, some people discover that they have an opponent in a boss, manager, or even the person working next to them.

In a game, having a rival to play against is a great motivator. It gives a team a common focus, a shared "enemy" to combine forces against to win. At a job, this competitive instinct can be good if it's productive. Rivalry can get your adrenaline—not to mention ideas—flowing.

However, when the enemy is someone within your company, the results are not productive. Instead of working together toward a common goal, colleagues often end up gossiping, complaining, and working against one another. This divisiveness can waste valuable time and energy that could be spent on getting the job done. It also creates a potentially stressful and unhappy work environment where trust may become an issue.

How Teams Work

Groups of people can work together in many different ways. There is no single model of a team. Instead, a team's organization will depend on many factors. These can range from the kind of business and where it is located to the needs and wants of owners and customers.

Some teams consist of people who all sit together in a common workspace. Throughout the day, they talk to one another about projects and deal with problems that come up. In other cases, people on the same team might sit in separate spaces and meet up once a day, once a week, or even once a month. They do their own thing but get together every once in a while to discuss projects and trade ideas.

Thanks to today's technology, many teams don't need to get together in person—in a conference room, for example, or by the water cooler—but can keep in touch via cell phones, e-mail, and conference calls. An increasing number of businesses count on "virtual teams." These people see each other very rarely. Although some team members might work in the same office building, others might live in different cities, states, or even countries.

Some teams discuss work in person. Thanks to the Internet and video conferencing, members of a team can just as easily be from the other side of the country.

Despite the various ways they are formed and operate, however, every team shares values and objectives, and team members all communicate with one another.

Team Motivation and Guidance

If the team you're part of is going to thrive, you and everyone else involved will have to stay motivated. Motivation occurs when people are kept interested and enthusiastic so they can meet their own individual goals as well as the common ones of the team.

How are people motivated? When a boss, manager, or company involves employees in the business's operations, it lets people know how important their contributions are and provides motivation. You, too, can guide your coworkers. Make them feel involved, and let them know that you take their thoughts and contributions seriously. Ask them how you can help them complete tasks that will meet your team's goals.

It is also important to make sure goals are clear. Sometimes, people on a team work so hard that they lose sight of the end result. From time to time, it's important to sit down and reevaluate goals and to review each person's role in achieving them. Sometimes, it helps to do this away from your work environment. Go somewhere where everyone can relax and let down their guard. It is often easier to examine how work relationships are functioning when you have an outside perspective. While it's crucial that you discuss any problems that are occurring between team members, it's also essential that you guide and encourage one another. High morale and confidence make a team successful.

chapter four

BEING ASSERTIVE AND INFLUENTIAL

Do you ever feel like you try too hard to be nice? Do you find yourself avoiding arguments or unpleasant confrontations? Do you have trouble expressing yourself, telling someone what you really want, or find yourself agreeing to do things or take on tasks that later you wish you hadn't?

From time to time, we all say or do things in order to please other people and then ask ourselves, "Why didn't I just say 'no'?," "Why didn't I stand up for myself?," or "Why didn't I say what I really think?" Of course, having a job means doing some things you don't necessarily always want to do. Aside from owing a manager or boss your respect, you need to try to comply with his or her rules and wishes. However, chances are you were hired for your job due to a combination of your personality, skills, and experience. And no matter what kind of job you have, it is important that you be allowed to communicate your ideas and display your talents in a productive manner. The skill of expressing yourself in a clear, honest, and positive way is known as being assertive.

Assertiveness vs. Aggressiveness

Some people confuse assertiveness with aggressiveness. Aggressiveness involves being hostile toward someone else. Oftentimes, when someone is being aggressive, he or she will use an argument that goes beyond the discussed topic or issue and attacks the other person's character. Assertiveness means standing up for yourself and what you believe is right. While you should consider other people's rights and feelings, you also want them to be aware of yours. Assertiveness involves letting people know what kind of treatment is acceptable to you and what isn't. It also has to do with taking responsibility, expressing yourself effectively, and wanting respect for your contributions, efforts, and ideas. In addition, assertiveness includes being able to stand up for yourself, actively disagree, express positive or negative feelings, and make requests.

Lack of Assertiveness

Lack of assertiveness can potentially cause problems. If you outwardly act as if everything is fine but inwardly you resent an authoritarian boss or a bullying coworker, these pent-up feelings can eat away at you. You may want to express your feelings but don't have the confidence to do so. Your anger might reach a boiling point. You might keep these feelings to yourself, which can be confusing and depressing. Or you could erupt, sometimes at the wrong place and time. For instance, you may end up unfairly taking out your anger on someone—a colleague or family member, for example—who has nothing to do

If you are upset about something at work but keep your feelings to yourself, your anger could come out at other times, perhaps with family or a friend.

with your work frustrations. You may even finally explode in front of your boss or coworker. However, having held in your feelings for so long, your reaction may seem out of proportion with the comparatively small but final straw that caused it.

Assertiveness Techniques

A lot of people mistakenly believe that being assertive means that one must be like a human bulldozer. But there are many ways to be assertive. You can be heard,

Are You Assertive?

If you are able to do the following, then you are asserting yourself. If not, you need to work on being more assertive:

- Express your feelings when a friend or coworker does something unkind or unreasonable
- Ask questions or express opinions without fearing that you won't be taken seriously
- Speak up about unfair treatment, too much work, or a policy or rule that you don't agree with
- Object when you feel you are being treated poorly
- Address a group without getting anxious
- Accept criticism without getting upset or defensive

understood, and respected, and (at times) get your way without losing your temper or control. Although you can't always be assertive and be nice, it doesn't mean you should be nasty.

One common assertiveness technique is called the three-part assertion message. Its aim is to convey your needs to another person and bring about a change in behavior. The first part of the message describes the offending behavior. The second part addresses how it affects you, and the third part focuses on how it makes you feel. For example, if a coworker is repeatedly late for a meeting, you could say something like: "When you are late for our meetings [this is the offending behavior], I waste time waiting for you that I could be spending on work [how it affects you]. This is frustrating for me [how it makes you feel], and I'd like us to work on solving the problem." This last part of the statement leads to finding a solution.

For some other assertiveness techniques, let's take the following scenario as an example: Your boss asks you to write a report. When you give it to him or her, your boss has a very negative reaction. You may feel terrible and at a loss. But there are ways that you can take charge of the situation:

Agreement

Boss: This report is terrible!

You: You're right. It is.

Boss: What do you mean, "It is"? It's full of grammar mistakes.

You: You're right, my grammar is awful.

Boss: Well, this is a problem.

You: You're right. I'm really bad at reports.

(Your boss isn't prepared for you to agree with him or her. By surprising your boss, you take control.)

Being Direct and Honest

Boss: You're useless! Once again, you've handed in a terrible report!

You: I don't like it when you attack me. I'd prefer if you let me know specifically what the problem is. Then we'll see what can be done to improve things.

A young woman discusses her work performance with her manager. After listening to her boss's feedback, the woman expresses her thoughts in a calm, clear manner.

(You let your boss see how you feel and then take charge of the situation by proposing that you work together to make it better.)

Negotiating

Boss: This report is terrible!
You: What's the matter with it?
Boss: It's full of errors.
You: Would you like me to do it over?
Boss: Yes. Have it back to me in three hours.
You: I need to finish another project first. But I can have it back to you tomorrow morning.

(This is a type of negotiation where both you and your boss end up winning. You both express yourselves and the report gets done.)

Depending on the situation, you can choose what reaction you feel is most appropriate and comfortable. For instance, some people might feel stress from thinking that they must get angry and stand their ground. Or they might not want to react negatively to an unfair or unkind comment. Often, more important than defeating your opponent is giving yourself the choice of how you react to a situation. You don't have to simply take whatever unfair treatment a coworker or boss is dishing out.

Influencing and Guiding Others

Influencing other people is similar to being assertive. At work, influential people are respected and admired by their colleagues and superiors. Furthermore, their ideas carry weight.

In some job situations, you will need to positively influence others. Inspiring and serving as a guide to colleagues is a form of influencing. So is winning their support so that they'll back you up on your projects or ideas. Being influential is important in that, no matter what you do, it makes your job a lot easier. People are naturally drawn to others who are positive, determined, considerate, and capable of expressing themselves well. Instead of complaining or wishing things were different, influential people figure out what needs doing. They then use the interpersonal skills at their disposal—verbal communication, body language, assertiveness, experience, and understanding of different situations and people—to guide others and get things done.

No Pressure

Just as assertiveness shouldn't be confused with aggressiveness, influencing people shouldn't be mistaken for forcing them into doing things your way. Bullying or nagging others to do something or see an issue from your point of view doesn't work. In fact, it will likely cause them to lose respect for you and even dislike you.

Truly successful influencers always take others' feelings and views into consideration. They understand that to guide others, they must be flexible and adapt their interpersonal skills to different contexts and types of people.

Consider the following example. An American tourist is visiting a country where no one understands

When you talk face-to-face, you have the other person's undivided attention. It is easier for him or her to hear you and to be persuaded by your point of view.

English. The tourist wants a hamburger. However, it won't matter how long or loud she screams, "I want a hamburger!" Nor will it matter how important, good-looking, or smart she is, or how much money she has. She can insist and threaten and plead, but because she doesn't speak the country's language, she's not going to get the hamburger. She has no influence whatsoever.

Similarly, if you want to influence or guide people in the workplace, you have to try to speak their language. This means figuring out the needs and wants of others. Then take these requirements and wishes into

Different Kinds of Influencing

There are many different ways of being influential and guiding others. Some people are good at influencing in certain contexts (face-to-face meetings, for example, or on the phone) but not in others (in front of a big audience or delivering a speech). A lucky and talented few are good in almost any context. There are four types of influential people that you're likely to find in any workplace:

- **Leaders:** Highly visible people who naturally attract attention. They are skilled at guiding others because they can set overall goals, and devise and communicate strategies to achieve them.
- **Internal influencers:** Work well within a group. They're great at bringing people together and guiding them toward a common goal. They do this by offering encouragement while balancing different people's skills and personalities.
- **One-on-one influencers:** Rely on their skills of being understanding, supportive, and gently persuasive to guide another person toward seeing and accepting new alternatives.
- **Issue influencers:** Often have a specific issue or cause about which they are passionate. Fueled by their strong beliefs and commitment, they try to inspire others and guide them toward accepting their views.

consideration in order to build bridges with others and win over allies. Despite differences, if people sense they have things in common—such as likes, dislikes, ideas, or goals—they're much more likely to be sympathetic to one another.

In a sense, we are all "foreigners." You might get frustrated that someone doesn't understand your point of view, but keep in mind that he or she too might be experiencing the same frustration. Instead of trying harder to get people to see things your way (like the shouting tourist), try changing tactics. You will likely get better results if you speak in encouraging tones, use plenty of eye contact, and invite people to state their opinions so they know you respect them. People will be more willing to meet you halfway if they feel that you appreciate their points of view. They may even agree to do something they wouldn't normally agree to because you have made them feel important.

chapter five

RESOLVING CONFLICTS

Few people like conflict. Being in a situation in which you're constantly arguing or being treated unfairly can be a major source of stress, frustration, and tension. Conflicts in the workplace can create an unpleasant atmosphere where it's hard to get work done and difficult to feel happy or enthusiastic. Therefore, it's important to learn the interpersonal skills that allow you to resolve conflicts when they arise.

Miscommunication

Conflict occurs in situations in which there is opposition. Opposition occurs when people disagree on a subject and can't find a solution. Often a solution can't be reached due to miscommunication. People can't agree if they're unable to understand each other's point of view. Misunderstandings can occur when people:

- Have different opinions or beliefs
- Come from different backgrounds or cultures

- Have emotional reactions to a person or issue
- Don't understand each other or communicate well

"It's Not My Fault!"

When miscommunication occurs, a natural reaction is to blame the other person. For instance, think of what happens if you're in a car or on a bike and you nearly have a collision with another vehicle. It doesn't matter whose fault it is. It is likely that your natural reaction is to scream or yell at the other person. Rarely, if ever, will you look at the way you yourself were driving.

In a conflict situation, our common reaction is to think that if the other person would change, everything would be resolved. "If my boss would just stop being so nitpicking and demanding, this job would be better." Or, "If my colleague would stop being such a know-it-all, it would ease the tension between us."

As the "difficult" person continues to complicate your work life, you may find yourself storing up accusations and resentment toward him or her. You might make up mental lists of how the person should change so there would be less conflict. You might even get to a point where you think the person is doing these annoying things on purpose, just to get to you.

Meanwhile, if you are so busy feeling slighted, you might be unable to look at the conflict with an objective eye. When you're feeling wronged by someone, you're not very likely to look at your own flaws. But take a step back and analyze the conflict. Although it may be tough, try to look at the other person's point of view. Is there

People often get so emotionally worked up during an argument that it's hard for them to express what they really want to say, let alone really listen to other people's viewpoints.

any way that that person could claim that you are being unreasonable, closed-minded, or difficult? Chances are that—rightly or wrongly—someone out there (whether a parent, sibling, friend, or work colleague) very likely finds you "difficult" at times as well.

The Wrong Way to Resolve a Conflict

When confronted with a conflict, most people will often react by doing one of the following:

- Avoiding the conflict as much as possible
- Trying not to make waves with the "difficult" person
- Storing up evidence of the "bad" things the other person does
- Complaining or gossiping about the person behind his or her back to people who seem sympathetic
- Getting into a big blowout with the person

Unfortunately, none of these techniques will help resolve conflicts or help you deal with difficult people. They might temporarily make you feel better, but they won't change the situation. They might even make it worse. By placing all the blame on the other person, you are making that person responsible for how you feel. In doing so, you're giving that person control over your relationship.

Better Ways of Resolving a Conflict

Despite how complicated or unpleasant a conflict may be, you always have a choice: either you become the other person's victim, or you try to take charge of the relationship. If you use your interpersonal skills effectively, you can manage the other person instead of allowing that person to manage you.

No matter how annoying, unfair, or mean you think someone else is, you can't count on that person to give his or her personality a makeover. What you can change, however, is the relationship—by changing how you act and what you say to this person. Although you may not always get what you want, you will be more in charge of what happens between the two of you.

Personal conflicts and arguments at work not only affect those directly involved, but everybody else at the office, too.

Negotiating

If two people or groups can't agree on how to resolve a disagreement, they have three options. They can walk away, get into a fight, or try to communicate in order to find a solution that works for both sides. Dealing with conflict through communication is known as negotiating.

Contrary to what many people believe, negotiation isn't about one person winning and the other losing. Rather, it's about both sides feeling as if they got something they wanted. Negotiations are successful when

Bullies

Bullies like to be in control and don't care about other people's feelings or opinions. Therefore, it can be nearly impossible to communicate your feelings. They would rather do what they want than negotiate. They don't apologize or back down. And bullies particularly enjoy picking on people they perceive as weak because it makes them feel even stronger.

Unfortunately, bullies can exist in the workplace, and they can make your life difficult if you let them. Intimidation, harassment, unfair criticism and blame, and being shouted at, bossed around, or unfairly singled out are all forms of bullying. More indirect types of bullying are also common. Bullying is any kind of behavior that has the goal of eating away at your confidence and self-esteem. As a result, you might dread going to work or be stressed, unmotivated, and less productive.

both sides leave discussions better off than when they first began. This is called a win-win situation. If one side feels better off but the other doesn't (a win-lose situation), the negotiation hasn't really been successful. You may have "won" this one time, but chances are the person or people you "defeated" won't want to negotiate with you ever again. They also won't trust you.

Negotiating can involve different kinds of skills and techniques. There is no one model. Instead, the approaches will depend upon the individuals and situations with which you are confronted. For instance, sometimes negotiating involves talking issues through. If everybody's individual interests are taken into consideration, then an agreement acceptable to all will likely be reached. At other times, successful negotiation involves

A job applicant smiles while responding to a question during an interview. People who show they are willing to negotiate have a better chance of getting a job.

give and take in which everybody has to give up one or more things they want.

No matter what the negotiation, however, you need to be flexible. Flexibility means you are able to see what your opponents want. Instead of stubbornly sticking to your position and refusing to budge, it might be better to give up one wish in exchange for another that you have a better chance of obtaining. Flexibility also means that when necessary, you can fight hard for something. But when the battle isn't worth it, you also are able to gracefully let it go.

Dealing with Difficult People

Sometimes, you'll run into conflicts where no resolution or negotiation is possible. This may be due to a variety of factors. In some cases, a person's behavior toward you may even be aggressive or discriminatory.

Workplaces have laws and rules that are designed to protect workers from discrimination and harassment. However, a lot of people find it difficult to make a formal complaint. Some people are afraid no one will believe them or that they'll lose their jobs. Others think that if they just let it go and do their work, eventually the person will leave them be.

It may be hard to stand up to someone who is harassing or abusing you in the workplace. However, if you don't confront him or her, the harassment will just continue. If you're already feeling low on self-esteem, face-to-face confrontation might seem overwhelming. Being assertive can be an effective tool. There are also other, less direct but still useful techniques for resolving, or at least improving, the situation.

Involve Others

If you are being harassed, discriminated against, or bullied, you may feel isolated from those around you. For this reason, don't keep the problem to yourself. Talk to someone such as a manager or human-resources person. Not only will this person have the skills and authority to deal with the offending person's behavior, but he or she also will be able to provide you with advice and support.

Be Objective

Being treated poorly and unfairly can leave you hurt, angry, and frustrated. However, when you talk to someone about what's going on, you should present the problem in a calm, rational manner. Instead of finger-pointing, offer particular examples of how you were treated and the consequences.

- **Nonobjective way:** "Jane hates me. Anytime I say something, she attacks me. She's just out to get me."
- **Objective way:** "I've been having difficulty with Jane. Yesterday, during a meeting, she criticized my work in front of everyone and wouldn't give me an opportunity to present my point of view. Unfortunately, these conflicts have come up at the last four meetings."

Calm Confrontation

People who bully, harass, and discriminate count on one of two reactions: silence or an outpouring of anger. If the victim is too scared to react and stays silent, the person feels he or she has triumphed. And if the victim loses his or her cool and strikes back, the bully will be thrilled to have provoked an explosion of sorts. Furthermore, playing rough is second nature to such people, since they are likely to win any kind of conflict.

For this reason, another good way to deal with difficult people is to confront them—but in a calm way that will take them by surprise. Instead of blaming them or losing your temper, refuse to play by their rules.

Temperamental way

Them: Your work is terrible! I don't know how you got hired.

You: Shut up! You think you're so great, but everybody here hates your guts.

(With a response like this, you'll likely just get into a lot of name-calling.)

Calm way

Them: Your work is terrible! I don't know how you got hired.

You: Your yelling at me isn't very productive. I'm disappointed that you can't sit down and have a discussion about how my work could be improved.

(Instead of launching into a fight, you are expressing how they let you down, while acknowledging that there is room for negotiating about any real problems they have with your work.)

Setting Boundaries

Letting people know how their behavior affects you is called boundary setting. Boundaries are limits. If you don't set clear boundaries—or if you say nothing at all—you are in a way saying that the way others treat you is OK.

When you set boundaries, you are taking charge. You are defining your relationship by communicating what kind of treatment is OK with you and what isn't. Even if the other person's attitude doesn't change all at once, over time he or she will know that you are not

10 Great Questions to Ask

1. Do I feel able to complain about too large a workload?

2. Am I able to express myself at work without fear of being viewed as stupid?

3. Am I able to stand up for my rights when a coworker is unreasonable or rude?

4. Do I make sure others understand the meaning of what I'm communicating by encouraging them to ask questions and make comments?

5. Am I always polite even when I disagree or don't like the person I'm dealing with?

6. Do I listen to other people's opinions and try to see an issue from their points of view (even if I don't necessarily agree with their positions)?

7. Am I a good negotiator?

8. Do I give my undivided attention to people with whom I'm speaking or corresponding?

9. Do I work well in a group or team?

10. Am I good at providing support and motivation to the people I work with?

When colleagues respect and communicate well with each other, spending time at work is a much more pleasurable experience.

going to accept certain types of behavior. From there, you can negotiate a different way of communicating.

Prepared for the Workplace

Ultimately, if you are able to learn and put into practice a wide variety of interpersonal skills, you will be well prepared for any workplace. The truth is that if you can't connect with the people you work with, it probably won't matter how hard you work or how many brilliant ideas you may have. You might be surprised to discover that many people with high IQs don't necessarily land the top jobs. The reason for this is that despite their intelligence, they often lack interpersonal skills. In fact, job experts have found that emotional intelligence—the capacity to manage your emotions well—is just as important to success in the workplace as a high IQ or lots of expertise.

Good interpersonal skills will help ensure day-to-day happiness at your job. They also will contribute significantly to your overall success—not only in the career that you choose but also in the life you lead.

glossary

adrenaline A burst of energy.

assertive Confident, self-assured.

authoritarian Expecting or imposing complete obedience.

boundaries Limits.

cause Ideal, goal, or movement to which a person or group is committed.

comply To agree with or act in accordance with rules, desires, or demands.

context The environment or situation in which an event takes place.

defensive Constantly protecting oneself against criticism (whether real or perceived) from others.

discrimination Prejudiced treatment or action against someone.

divisiveness Creation of disunity or disagreement.

flexible Willing or open to change (of positions, attitudes, or point of view).

harass To continually disturb, bother, harm, or torment someone.

harmonious In agreement.

inflection The pitch and level of volume of a voice.

influence To have an effect on or indirectly bring about change.

issue A point, matter, or dispute of public importance.

morale Mental or emotional condition—such as enthusiasm, confidence, or loyalty—of an individual or group. Also, a sense of common purpose within a group.

motivated Encouraged, stimulated.

negotiate To attempt to come to an agreement through discussion and compromise.

perspective An evaluation of a situation or facts from an objective point of view.

productive Bringing about results, benefits, or profits.

reevaluate Reconsider.

relationship management The skill of dealing positively with others in terms of personal and work relationships.

slighted Treated with indifference.

tone Style or manner of expression.

unambiguous Clear and precise.

virtual Carried on by means of a computer or computer system (for example, the Internet).

Career Kids, LLC
5043 Gregg Way
Auburn, CA 95602
(800) 537-0909
Web site: http://careerkids.com/index.html
Career Kids offers books, videos, resume tips, and other
materials for teens, covering all aspects of choosing
a career and finding a job.

DO-IT (Disabilities, Opportunities, Internetworking, and
Technology)
University of Washington
Box 355670
Seattle, WA 98195-5670
(888) 972-DOIT (3648) or (206) 685-DOIT (3648)
Web site: http://www.washington.edu/doit
DO-IT helps people with disabilities get into challenging
academic programs and careers, with the support of
computer and networking technologies that
increase productivity and independence.

The Emily Post Institute, Inc.
444 South Union Street
Burlington, VT 05401
Web site: http://www.emilypost.com/business/index.htm
Created by Emily Post in 1946 and run today by third-
generation family members, the Emily Post Institute
is dedicated to teaching social and business skills as
well as manners for every occasion.

Service Canada
Employment Information Services
140 Promenade du Portage
Phase IV, 5th Floor, Box 511
Gatineau, QC K1A 0J9
Canada
(800) 827-0271
Web site: http://jobbank.gc.ca/Intro_en.aspx
The Canadian government offers information related to
    all aspects of employment in Canada, including
    career information and job tips for youths and stu-
    dents. The Service Canada Job Bank is the largest
    Web-based job network in the nation.

U.S. Bureau of Labor Statistics (BLS)
Postal Square Building
2 Massachusetts Avenue NE
Washington, DC 20212-0001
(202) 691-5200
Web site: http://www.bls.gov/k12
The BLS provides up-to-date information and statistics
    about every kind of job and career. Its teen-specific
    Web site includes a wealth of information about
    possible career paths.

Youth2Work
U.S. Department of Labor
Frances Perkins Building
200 Constitution Avenue NW
Washington, DC 20210
(866) 4-USA-DOL (487-2365)

Web site: http://www.youth2work.gov/index.htm
This section of the U.S. Department of Labor focuses on
    labor laws, worker safety, and career options for
    teens in the workplace.

Web Sites

Due to the changing nature of Internet links, Rosen
Publishing has developed an online list of Web sites
related to the subject of this book. This site is updated
regularly. Please use this link to access the list:

http://www.rosenlinks.com/wr/insk

Badegruber, Bernie. *101 More Life Skills Games for Children: Learning, Growing, Getting Along (Ages 9–15)*. Alameda, CA: Hunter House, 2006.

Bolles, Richard Nelson, et al. *What Color Is Your Parachute for Teens: Discovering Yourself, Defining Your Future*. Berkeley, CA: Ten Speed Press, 2006.

Drew, Naomi, M.A. *The Kids' Guide to Working Out Conflicts: How to Keep Cool, Stay Safe, and Get Along*. Minneapolis, MN: Free Spirit Publishing, 2004.

Kalman, Izzy. *Bullies to Buddies: How to Turn Your Enemies into Friends*. Staten Island, NY: Wisdom Pages, 2005.

Kaufman, Gershen, et al. *Stick Up for Yourself! Every Kid's Guide to Personal Power and Positive Self-Esteem*. Minneapolis, MN: Free Spirit Publishing, 1999.

Moore, June Hines. *Social Skills Survival Guide: A Handbook for Interpersonal and Business Etiquette*. Nashville, TN: Broadman & Holman Publishers, 2003.

Shipley, David, and Will Schwalbe. *Send: The Essential Guide to Email for Office and Home*. New York, NY: Alfred A. Knopf, 2007.

bibliography

"Ability to Delegate: Interview Questions." JobBank USA. Retrieved May 2007 (http://www.jobbankusa.com/interview_questions_answers/free_samples_examples/ability_to_delegate.html).

"Developing Interpersonal Skills." Career Services. Seneca College of Applied Arts & Technology. Retrieved May 2007 (http://ilearn.senecac.on.ca/careers/succeed/developing.html).

Impact Factory. Retrieved May 2007 (http://www.impactfactory.com).

"The Importance of Interpersonal Skills." The Open University. OpenLearn: Learning Space. Retrieved May 2007 (http://openlearn.open.ac.uk/mod/resource/view.php?id=108488).

"Interpersonal Skills." Key Skills. Canterbury Christ Church University. Retrieved May 2007 (http://keyskills.cant.ac.uk/wto/index.htm).

MacMullin, Colin. "Communication and Counselling for Humanitarian Workers, Part 4: Assertiveness: Communicating Your Own Ideas and Feelings." The Refugee Experience. Retrieved June 2007 (http://earlybird.qeh.ox.ac.uk/rfgexp/rsp_tre/student/comcoun/cou_05.htm).

Shipley, David, and Will Schwalbe. *Send: The Essential Guide to Email for Office and Home*. New York, NY: Alfred A. Knopf, 2007.

"Teaching/Learning Toolkit." Equipped for the Future Center for Training and Technical Assistance. Retrieved May 2007 (http://eff.cls.utk.edu/toolkit/standards_wheel.htm).

"Ten Ways to Improve Your Interpersonal Skills." AllBusiness.com. Retrieved June 2007

(http://www.allbusiness.com/human-resources/
careers-career-development/11134-1.html).
Van Wagner, Kendra. "Types of Nonverbal
Communication." About.com: Psychology.
Retrieved June 2007 (http://psychology.about.com/
od/nonverbalcommunication/a/nonverbaltypes.htm).

index

About the Author

Michael A. Sommers was born in Texas and raised in Canada. After earning a bachelor's degree in English literature at McGill University in Montreal, Canada, he completed a master's degree in history and civilizations from the École des Hautes Études en Sciences Sociales in Paris, France. For the last fifteen years, he has worked as a writer and photographer. His numerous books for Rosen include various career-related titles, such as *Cool Careers Without College for People Who Love Homes*, *Cool Careers Without College for People Who Love to Buy Things*, and *Wildlife Photographer: Life Through a Lens*.

Photo Credits

Cover (top, left to right) © istockphoto.com, © istockphoto.com/ Dagmar Heymans, © istockphoto.com/Nancy Louie; cover (middle) © istockphoto.com; cover (bottom, left to right) © istockphoto.com/Diane Diederich, © Shutterstock, © istockphoto. com/Trista Weibell; pp. 7, 17, 25, 31, 42 (left to right) © www. istockphoto.com, © www.istockphoto.com/Diane Diederich, © www.istockphoto.com/Nancy Louie; p. 8 © www.istockphoto.com/ Jeffrey Smith; p. 9 © www.istockphoto.com/Tom Gulfer; p. 11 © www.istockphoto.com/Mike Manzano; p. 13 © istockphoto.com/ Mark Goddard; p. 14 © Dwayne Newton/Photo Edit; p. 19 © White Packert/Getty Images; p. 20 © www.istockphoto.com/Jaimie Duplass; p. 22 © www.istockphoto.com/Sean Locke; pp. 26, 29, 39 © Shutterstock; p. 33 © Bonnie Kamin/Photo Edit; p. 36 © Michael Newman/Photo Edit; pp. 44, 53 © www.istockphoto.com; p. 46 © www.istockphoto.com/Renne Lee; p. 48 © Getty Images.

Designer: Nelson Sá; **Photo Researcher:** Marty Levick